The Read and Learn Series: Book One

Read 50

50-Word Reading Passages
for
Fact, Fiction, and Fun
at the
600-Word Level

Andrew E. Bennett

PRO LINGUA ASSOCIATES

Pro Lingua Associates, Publishers

P.O. Box 1348, Brattleboro, Vermont 05302 USA
Office: 802 257 7779 • Orders: 800 366 4775
Email: info@ProLinguaAssociates.com
WebStore: www.ProLinguaAssociates.com
SAN: 216-0579

*At Pro Lingua
our objective is to foster an approach
to learning and teaching that we call
interplay, the interaction of language
learners and teachers with their materials,
with the language and culture,
and with each other in active, creative,
and productive play.*

ISBN 0-86647-226-6

This book was written and designed by Andrew E. Bennett. The Read & Learn edition was adapted for Pro Lingua by Raymond C. Clark. The design was adjusted by Arthur A. Burrows. It was printed and bound by Worzalla in Stevens Point, Wisconsin.

Cover by James Borstein, Corporate Communications: Targeted Graphics and Design

Image Credits:

Andrew E. Bennett: pp. 30, 44 (© Andrew E. Bennett)
Idea Design Center: pp. 4 (left), 74 (© Idea Design Center)
iStock Photos: pp. 4 (right), 10, 12, 14 18, 22, 24, 26 (bottom left, bottom right (top right, bottom)), 34, 36, 38, 52, 54, 56, 58, 60, 62, 64, 66, 68, 70, 76, 78, 80 (© iStock Photos)
Very Image: p. 5 (© Very Image)
Sam: p. 6 (© Andrew E. Bennett)
Xiao Peng: pp. 8, 48 (© Andrew E. Bennett)
Hemera/Big Box of Art: p. 20, 26 (top left, top right, bottom right (top left)), 56 (© Hemera)
John Stephens: p. 28 (used with permission) (© John Stephens)
DJ Soft: pp. 32, 46 (© Dance & Jump Software)
Q Vision: pp. 2, 40 (© Q Vision Co.)
Grace Kuo: p. 42 (© Andrew E. Bennett)
Dainippon: p. 50 (© Dainippon Screen MFG Co.)
E&A: pp. 51 (A, B, D), 72 (© E&A Digital Arts)
Corel: pp. 51 (C), 56 (gate) (© Corel)

Printed in the United States of America.
First edition. First Printing 2006. 2,000 copies in print.

Contents

Welcome --1

Unit 1   The Amazon River --2

Unit 2   Jennifer's Seasons ---4

Unit 3   Yo-Yo Ma ---6

Unit 4   Where am I?---8

Unit 5   Popcorn --10

Unit 6   The Noisy People---12

Unit 7   Mount Fuji ---14

Unit 8   What People Drink---16

Unit 9   Blogs --18

Unit 10   Buying Movie Tickets --------------------------------------20

Unit 11   The Great Barrier Reef-------------------------------------22

Unit 12   Ways to Spend the Weekend--------------------------------24

Unit 13   Building a Model --26

Unit 14   Digital Art ---28

Unit 15   Email: How's it going? -------------------------------------30

Unit 16   Chimpanzees ---32

Unit 17   New York City - Event Guide ------------------------------34

Unit 18   Interview with a Fire Fighter ------------------------------36

Unit 19   This Old Car ---38

Unit 20   Cinco de Mayo --40

Contents

Unit 21   Map of Jefferson County ---------------------------------------42

Unit 22   Profile of a Computer Expert -------------------------------44

Unit 23   Thank You Note--46

Unit 24   Meeting a Foreign Exchange Student --------------------48

Unit 25   Space Dreams--50

Unit 26   The Iditarod ---52

Unit 27   Junk Food---54

Unit 28   Movie Posters ---56

Unit 29   What do you think?--58

Unit 30   Hurricanes ---60

Unit 31   Being a Good Language Learner -----------------------------62

Unit 32   The Knowledge ---64

Unit 33   My Mother --66

Unit 34   Making Chocolate Chip Cookies ----------------------------68

Unit 35   Internet Chatroom: Christmas Shopping ----------------70

Unit 36   Skateboarding --72

Unit 37   Saturday is my day!--74

Unit 38   The Calgary Stampede --76

Unit 39   MP3 Players--78

Unit 40   Oil ---80

Answer Key ---82

For the Teacher ---90

Dear Reader,

Welcome to Book One in the Read and Learn Series. You can read about the world we live in -- our home and the places in it. You can read about the things we do -- work, play, travel, study, shop, talk, email, and eat. And you can learn a lot of useful English.

There are 40 units in this book. Each unit has a reading and three exercises. The units are easy to do.

- Do the reading
- Do the exercises
- Check your answers (the answers start on page 82)

But first, you should understand these instructions before you begin to work.

_____ Write the correct word in each blank.

_____ Choose the best answer.

_____ Put the words in the correct order.

_____ Complete each sentence.

_____ Match each question with the correct answer.

_____ Match each sentence with a response.

_____ Combine the two sentences into one sentence.

Now, read and learn and enjoy the book.

Pro Lingua Associates

The Amazon River is 4,000 miles long (6,400 kilometers). It's the world's second longest. It's also the home of many plants, animals, and fish.

The Amazon begins in five different countries in South America. It's a big river with many secrets. We're still learning about them.

Vocabulary

Write the correct word in each blank.

long	many	big	also	secret

1. There are _____ people in the park.

2. You should tell Jim about the party. You should _____ tell Carla.

3. Your hair is so _____! Does it take long to wash?

4. Sorry, I can't tell you. It's a _____.

Reading

Choose the best answer.

1. (   ) How many countries does the Amazon begin in?
      A: 2.
      B: 5.
      C: 4,000.
      D: 6,400.

2. (   ) The Amazon is not full of _____.
      A: people   B: fish
      C: animals   D: plants

3. (   ) What is probably true?
      A: We know everything about the Amazon.
      B: We can't learn anything more about the Amazon.
      C: There are not many fish in the Amazon.
      D: It takes time to learn all about the Amazon.

4. (   ) Which of these is true?
      A: The Amazon is 6,400 miles long.
      B: The Amazon begins in more than one country.
      C: The Amazon is the longest river.
      D: The Amazon is in North America.

Grammar

Put the words in the correct order.

1. South country not America is a

_____.

2. in there many the fish river Are

_____?

3. biggest is It world's the country

_____.

2 Jennifer's Seasons

In the spring, I spend a lot of time outside. I like smelling the new flowers.

In the summer, I often go to the beach. I also eat a lot of ice cream.

In the fall, I like picking apples. Fresh apples taste great!

In the winter, I usually stay inside. Sometimes, I go to the mall.

Vocabulary

Write the correct word in each blank.

smells	summer	often	inside	winter

1. In the _____, many places are cold.

2. That _____ great! What are you cooking?

3. Don't let the dog _____. He's dirty.

4. It _____ rains here. It's very rainy.

Reading

Choose the best answer.

1. (   ) When does Jennifer like cold desserts?
   A: In the spring.   B: In the summer.
   C: In the fall.   D: In the winter.

2. (   ) Jennifer likes to pick apples. What does this suggest?
   A: There may be an apple farm near Jennifer's house.
   B: Jennifer picks fresh apples every season.
   C: Apples taste great with ice cream.
   D: Apples are very popular in her country.

3. (   ) Which of these is **not** true?
   A: Jennifer likes going outside in the winter.
   B: In several seasons, Jennifer likes going out.
   C: Fresh flowers smell nice to Jennifer.
   D: Jennifer goes to a mall from time to time.

4. Which of these might be Jennifer in the summer?

A: B: C: D:

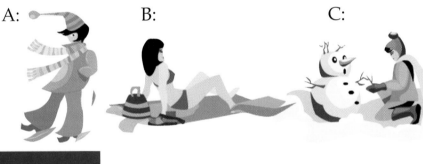

Grammar

Put the words in the correct order.

1. outside in She fall the time spends

   _____.

2. swim the We in summer

   _____.

3. like ice cream I to eat

   _____.

4. smell flowers The spring great

   _____.

3 Yo-Yo Ma

Yo-Yo Ma is a cello player. He gives concerts around the world. Sometimes he plays on TV shows. He has also made many music CDs.

Yo-Yo Ma plays with a lot of feeling. People love to hear him play. And he is very friendly with his fans.

Vocabulary

Write the correct word in each blank.

| around | music | play | friendly | world |

1. My uncle is very _____. Everybody likes him.

2. You _____ the piano very well!

3. Let's walk _____ the city for a while.

4. What kind of _____ do you like? I like rock.

Choose the best answer.

1. (   ) Yo-Yo Ma gives concerts _____.
   A: in many countries   B: in the USA only
   C: in other worlds   D: in just a few places

2. (   ) How does Yo-Yo Ma feel about his fans?
   A: He doesn't like them.
   B: He likes them.
   C: He knows them.
   D: He plays for them.

3. (   ) Why do people like Yo-Yo Ma?
   A: He is very friendly.
   B: He plays the cello.
   C: He gives many concerts.
   D: He makes CDs.

4. (   ) People _____.
   A: are very friendly
   B: love to hear him
   C: have a lot of feeling
   D: give many concerts

Grammar

Complete each sentence with *he*, *his*, or *him*.

1. Is this _____ CD?

2. Jack is my best friend. _____ lives near me.

3. Don't talk to _____. He is angry.

4. That's _____ cello. It's very old.

7

4   Where Am I?

Vocabulary

Write the correct word or words in each blank.

library	other	look for	lost	walk

1. I can't find my glasses. Help me _____ them.

2. Don't use that chair. Sit in the _____ one.

3. You can study at a _____.

4. I like to _____ to school. It takes about 20 minutes.

Reading

Choose the best answer.

1. (　) Where does the man talk to the woman?
  A: At the library. B: In the park.
  C: On 5th Street. D: On Blossom Avenue.

2. (　) The woman is _____ the man.
  A: helpful to B: afraid of
  C: old friends with D: unkind to

3. (　) Look at the map. Where is the library?

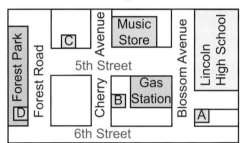

4. (　) Look at the map. Where should the man turn left?

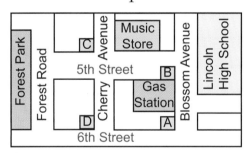

Grammar

Complete each sentence with *am, is,* or *are*.

1. There _____ a hotel near the park.

2. _____ I on Forest Road?

3. We _____ not near the library.

4. _____ there a gas station on 5th Street?

9

Popcorn is a great snack. It's easy to make and fun to eat. People love to eat it at the movies. It's also a popular snack to make at home. It takes only a few minutes.

Some people eat popcorn plain. Others like to add things to it, like butter and salt.

Vocabulary

Write the correct word in each blank.

movie	top	plain	eat	a few

1. There are only _____ people here. Where are the others?

2. Let's have dinner and see a _____ tonight.

3. What do you want to _____ for breakfast?

4. These clothes are very _____. They have no color.

Choose the best answer.

1. (   ) People like to eat popcorn _____.
    A: at restaurants
    B: at snack shops
    C: at movie theaters
    D: at work

2. (   ) Making popcorn _____.
    A: is not hard to do.
    B: takes a long time.
    C: is not easy to do at home.
    D: is a lot of trouble.

3. (   ) People do **not** eat popcorn _____.
    A: plain   B: with dinner
    C: with salt   D: with butter

4. (   ) Which of these is true?
    A: It takes a few hours to make popcorn.
    B: At the movies, only a few people eat popcorn.
    C: People like to make popcorn at the movies.
    D: Some people eat popcorn with butter.

Grammar

Put the words in the correct order.

1. easy it to Is make

   _____?

2. at eat People the it movies

   _____.

3. a snack very popular It is

   _____.

4. fun at home 's It to eat

   _____.

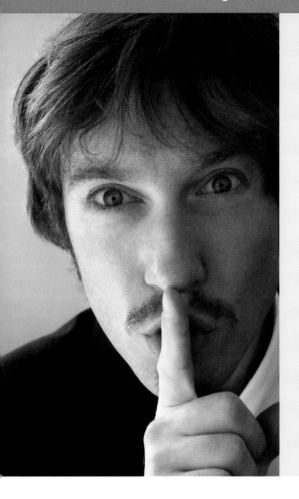

Jacob and his family ___(1)___ at a restaurant. They're enjoying a good ___(2)___. So are many other people.

Three people walk in. ___(3)___ They don't care about anyone else. They even laugh ___(4)___ monkeys! Jacob says, "People should be more polite." His family members agree.

Vocabulary

Write the correct word in each blank.

agree	anyone	polite	laugh	even

1. Hello? Is _____ home?

2. Sorry, but I don't _____. I have a different idea.

3. Funny movies make me _____.

4. Students should be _____ to their teachers.

Reading

Choose the best answer.

1. (　)　A: is
   B: they are
   C: are
   D: being

2. (　)　A: meal
   B: movie
   C: story
   D: way

3. (　)　A: They're very quiet.
   B: They quickly leave.
   C: They make friends with everyone.
   D: They sit down and start talking loudly.

4. (　)　A: as
   B: like
   C: for
   D: almost

Grammar

Complete each sentence with *am, is* or *are*.

1. They _____ making a lot of noise.

2. We _____ eating in a restaurant.

3. Jacob _____ not enjoying his dinner.

4. I _____ not laughing at those people.

7　Mount Fuji

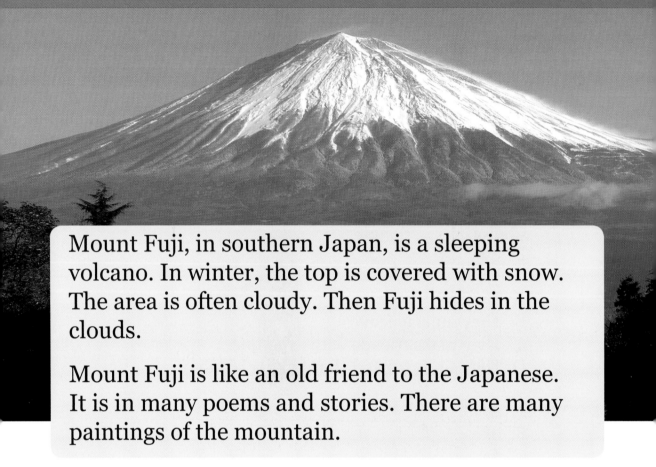

Mount Fuji, in southern Japan, is a sleeping volcano. In winter, the top is covered with snow. The area is often cloudy. Then Fuji hides in the clouds.

Mount Fuji is like an old friend to the Japanese. It is in many poems and stories. There are many paintings of the mountain.

Vocabulary

Write the correct word in each blank.

cover	hide	snow	painting	cloudy

1. I don't like _____. It's cold and wet!

2. It's really _____ today. I can't see the sun.

3. This _____ is my favorite. I love the dark colors.

4. My cat likes to _____ in here. Sometimes I can't find her!

Choose the best answer.

1. (   ) When is it hard to see Mount Fuji?
   A: In winter.
   B: In cloudy weather.
   C: When it has snow on top.
   D: When the weather is sunny.

2. (   ) The article does **not** say Mount Fuji is in many _____.
   A: stories
   B: paintings
   C: poems
   D: movies

3. (   ) What does "it" mean in the second paragraph?
   A: Japan   B: your best friend
   C: Mount Fuji   D: a volcano

4. (   ) What does the article say about the Japanese?
   A: They are bothered by Mount Fuji.
   B: They worry about Mount Fuji.
   C: They write about Mount Fuji.
   D: They don't like Mount Fuji.

Grammar

Put the words in the correct order.

1. snow mountain The covered is with

   _____.

2. today isn't cloudy It very

   _____.

3. about poems Fuji there many Are

   _____?

4. she an friend Is old

   _____?

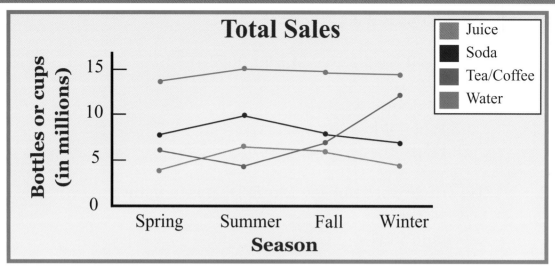

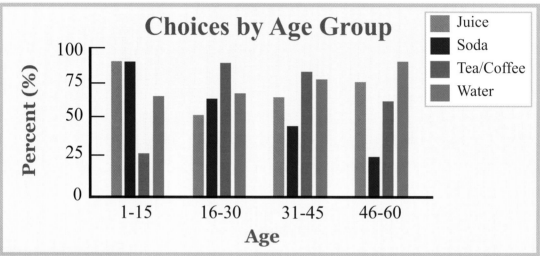

Vocabulary

Write the correct word in each blank.

common	spring	total	age	water

1. Write your name, _____, and address on the form.

2. What is the _____ cost of the food and drinks?

3. There's _____ on the floor. Can you clean it up?

4. The leaves and flowers are growing again. _____ is here!

Reading

Choose the best answer.

1. (   ) In summer, _____ bottles of soda are sold.
   A: 2 million
   B: 4 million
   C: 6 million
   D: 10 million

2. (   ) Which drink sales change the least season by season?
   A: Juice.   B: Soda.
   C: Tea/Coffee.   D: Water.

3. (   ) Which age group prefers coffee or tea the most?
   A: 1-15.   B: 16-30.
   C: 31-45.   D: 46-60.

4. (   ) Which of these is true?
   A: People aged 1-15 prefer to drink coffee or tea.
   B: Older people prefer water.
   C: 75% of people aged 31-45 like to drink soda.
   D: Less than 50% of all people like to drink juice.

Grammar

Write the correct word in each blank.

1. _____ do you like juice?

   (Why/How)

2. _____ water do they drink in winter?

   (How much/When)

3. _____ do people drink a lot of soda?

   (What/When)

4. _____ drink does she like?

   (What/Why)

9   Blogs

Blogs are like diaries on the Internet. In blogs, people write about their lives, schools, and jobs.

It's easy to start a blog, and it's free. You can add words and pictures to your blog any time. Just be careful. On the Internet, anybody can read your blog!

Vocabulary

Write the correct word in each blank.

Internet	add	careful	school	read

1. On the _____, I send and read emails.

2. Be _____ on that street. It's very dark.

3. Don't _____ that letter! It's mine!

4. There are about 1,000 students in my _____.

Choose the best answer.

1. (   ) To start a blog, you need a _____.
       A: diary
       B: book
       C: computer
       D: job

2. (   ) The article says blogs _____.
       A: are hard to start   B: don't cost any money
       C: are careful things   D: are usually about work

3. (   ) Why are blogs like diaries?
       A: They're both on the Internet.
       B: They're both open to anybody.
       C: Blogs and diaries take all of our time.
       D: You can write in them any time.

4. (   ) Which of these is **not** true?
       A: It's expensive to start a blog.
       B: You can put pictures on your blog.
       C: You can add to your blog every day.
       D: In blogs, people write about many things.

Grammar

Match each question with the correct answer.

1. __ Do you have a blog?	**A.** No, it doesn't.
2. __ Does he write poems?	**B.** No, she doesn't.
3. __ Does she read your blog?	**C.** Yes, I do.
4. __ Does it have pictures?	**D.** Yes, he does.

10 Buying Movie Tickets

Cashier: May I help you?

Customer: Yes, two tickets for *The Big Find*, please.

Cashier: For the 3:30 show?

Customer: Yes, that's right.

Cashier: We have a ticket deal. For $20, you can get two movie tickets, two drinks, and two bags of popcorn.

Customer: Sure, that's a good deal. Here's $50.

Cashier: Thank you. $30 is your change.

Vocabulary

Write the correct word in each blank.

ticket	get	change	help	right

1. On Mondays, you can _____ two drinks for $1.

2. This job is hard. Can you _____ me with it?

3. Yes, you're _____. Dogs cannot come in here.

4. Keep your _____. You need it to go inside.

Choose the best answer.

1. (   ) The cashier is _____ to the customer.
   A: helpful   B: unkind
   C: rude   D: right

2. (   ) The customer gets _____ thing(s) to eat and drink.
   A: one   B: two
   C: three   D: four

3. (   ) A ticket deal for six people would cost _____.
   A: $20
   B: $30
   C: $50
   D: $60

4. (   ) The customer says, "Sure, that's a good deal." What does
   he mean?
   A: The cashier is kind.
   B: The food is delicious.
   C: The price is good.
   D: The cashier is very smart.

Grammar

Put the words in the correct order.

1. change your is Here

   _____.

2. Are tickets the dollars twenty

   _____?

3. a That not deal good is

   _____!

11 The Great Barrier Reef

The Great Barrier Reef is one of the world's treasures. It is in northeast Australia. The Reef is more than 2,000 kilometers long. It is the home of thousands of coral reefs.

Visitors to Australia love to go to the Reef. They swim around carefully. They look at the beautiful fish, plants, and sea animals.

Vocabulary

Write the correct word in each blank.

beautiful	home	plant	fish	swim

1. At _____, I don't like to think about work.

2. Many people raise _____ as pets.

3. We _____ in the morning. It's our exercise for the day.

4. What a _____ day! Let's go for a walk.

Choose the best answer.

1. (　) The Great Barrier Reef is _____.
   - A: something every country has
   - B: popular with tourists
   - C: very common in the world
   - D: thousands of kilometers high

2. (　) What does the article say about Reef visitors? They _____.
   - A: swim carefully
   - B: can catch and eat the fish
   - C: are mostly from Australia
   - D: look for gold

3. (　) The Great Barrier Reef probably gets its name from _____.
   - A: its fish
   - B: its sea animals
   - C: its coral reefs
   - D: its sea plants

4. (　) What **don't** you find in the Great Barrier Reef?
   - A: Swimming tourists.　B: Golden treasure.
   - C: Beautiful fish.　　D: Coral reefs.

Grammar

Match each sentence with the correct reason.

1. ___ Please drive carefully.　**A.** We're in a hospital.

2. ___ Please be quiet.　**B.** It's late.

3. ___ Do it quickly.　**C.** The weather is bad.

4. ___ Wake up!　**D.** I want go home.

12 Ways to Spend the Weekend

Tina has two days off each week: Saturday and Sunday. She likes to read the newspaper one morning. The other morning, she goes jogging.

On weekend afternoons, Tina sees friends or talks on the phone.

At night, Tina likes going to nice restaurants and seeing shows. But those things are expensive. She can only choose one of them each week.

Vocabulary

Write the correct word in each blank.

phone	expensive	choose	morning	restaurant

1. We have breakfast together every _____.

2. Those things are __e_____. Be careful with them.

3. I have to go. Can I give you a(n) _____ call later?

4. Help me _____ a shirt to wear.

Reading

Choose the best answer.

1. ( ) On Saturday at 3:30 p.m., Tina might _____.
   A: read something   B: exercise
   C: talk to her best friend   D: see a show

2. ( ) On one weekend, Tina **cannot** _____.
   A: go jogging and talk on the phone
   B: go to a restaurant and see a show
   C: talk to friends and eat at a restaurant
   D: talk on the phone and see a show

3. ( ) Today is Saturday. Tina is reading a newspaper. What might Tina do the next morning?
   A: Read the newspaper again. B: Go jogging.
   C: Wake up late.   D: See a friend.

4. ( ) What could be Tina's schedule on a Saturday?

A:

Morning
Read the paper
Afternoon
See friends
Night
Go jogging

B:

Morning
Go jogging
Afternoon
Talk on the phone
Night
See a show

C:

Morning
Go jogging
Afternoon
See friends
Night
Read the paper

D:

Morning
See friends
Afternoon
Talk on the phone
Night
Go to a restaurant

Grammar

Put the words in the correct order.

1. to weekend on like I relax the

   _____.

2. it night cold get Does at very here

   _____?

3. morning She see the friends doesn't in

   _____.

4. sleeps mother an hour My the afternoon for in

   _____.

13 Building a Model

1. First, choose a model to build. Cars, trains, boats, and airplanes are popular kinds.

2. Next, find a place to build your model. It should be a clean area.

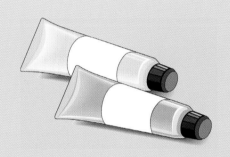

3. Then read the instructions carefully. Use special glue to put the pieces together.

4. Finally, paint your model. Use any colors you like!

Vocabulary

Write the correct word in each blank.

glue	build	finally	should	train

1. The road is closed. What _____ we do?

2. I can fix the lamp. Hand me the _____, please.

3. The _____ goes along the ocean. It's a lovely ride.

4. It's a big river. Can they really _____ a bridge across it?

Choose the best answer.

1. (   ) Which of these comes last?
   A: Choosing the model.
   B: Putting the model together.
   C: Painting the model.
   D: Finding a place to build the model.

2. (   ) The article does **not** mention model _____.
   A: boats   B: houses
   C: cars   D: trains

3. (   ) Which of these would be best for model building?
   A: A dirty table.
   B: A desk with books on it.
   C: A large, empty desk.
   D: The living room floor.

4. (   ) Which of these is true?
   A: You can use any kind of glue for a model.
   B: There are many kinds of popular models.
   C: It's OK to have a dirty building space.
   D: Models should all be the same color.

Grammar

Put the words in the correct order.

1. find place good a to Let's work

   _____.

2. instructions we Shall now read the

   _____?

3. not that use Let's glue

   _____.

4. paint boat Let's our red

   _____.

14 Digital Art

Digital Paint, by John Stephens

Digital art is made on computers. Artists use different computer programs. Some are good for drawing things. Others are good for adding color.

Becoming a good artist takes time and skill. Artists study hard to learn many programs. Finishing a job can take a long time. One piece may take 100 hours or more.

Vocabulary

Write the correct word in each blank.

hour	learn	color	draw	artist

1. What _____ should I paint my house?

2. I have to wash my clothes. It should take about a(n) _____.

3. I want to _____ Spanish. It's an important language.

4. Theresa is a(n) _____. Her work is beautiful.

Reading

Choose the best answer.

1. (　) Digital artists _____.
   A: all use the same programs　B: always finish jobs quickly
   C: need to have skill　　　　　D: don't need a computer

2. (　) What does the article say about computer programs?
   A: They're expensive.
   B: They're easy to learn.
   C: They all have the same uses.
   D: They have different uses.

3. (　) How can you become a digital artist?
   A: Draw a lot with a pen and paper.
   B: Work hard to learn programs.
   C: Spend 100 hours learning about art.
   D: Find a person with time and skill.

4. (　) In the second paragraph, what does "a job" mean?
   A: a piece of digital art
   B: a way to make a lot of money
   C: something about computers
   D: a class for learning digital art

Grammar

Put the words in the correct order.

1. Using fun is computers of a lot

   _____.

2. color takes time Adding lot of a

   _____.

3. easy isn't Becoming artist an

   _____.

4. also the Finishing work time takes

   _____.

15 Email: How's it going?

To: pedro_alarcon@yahoo.com

From: manny2004@hotmail.com

Subject: Hey there!

Hi Pedro!

How's your summer going? I'm having a great time __(1)__ my aunt's house. She __(2)__ computer. So I go onto the Internet every day. Sometimes I play basketball or go swimming. :-)

School starts in __(3)__ weeks. I know, I know…

I shouldn't __(4)__ about it! :-(

Well, see you soon!

Manny

Vocabulary

Write the correct word in each blank.

soon	every	great	week	know

1. Do you _____ the name of the company?

2. This is a(n) _____ song. I want to buy the CD.

3. It's late. We should leave _____.

4. I eat breakfast here _____ day.

Reading

Choose the best answer.

1. (   )   A: on
            B: at
            C: to
            D: from

2. (   )   A: needs a
            B: doesn't have a
            C: wants an old
            D: has a new

3. (   )   A: one
            B: the
            C: a few
            D: next

4. (   )   A: think
            B: know
            C: like
            D: work

Grammar

Match each sentence with a response.

1. ___ How's it going?   **A.** Good idea.

2. ___ Let's go swimming.   **B.** Bye bye.

3. ___ See you later.   **C.** Not bad.

4. ___ I like basketball.   **D.** Me, too.

16 Chimpanzees

Chimpanzees are very smart animals. They can solve many problems. They can also make and use tools.

Chimps live in groups. There are from 2 to 80 animals in a group. During the day, they find food together. They like to eat fruits and leaves. At night, chimps sleep in trees.

Vocabulary

Write the correct word in each blank.

live	make	group	smart	problem

1. There are four people in our _____.

2. It's a big _____. Can you solve it?

3. I like to _____ in the city. It's so exciting!

4. Tina loves to _____ soup. She eats it almost every day.

Choose the best answer.

1. (   ) How do chimps find food?
        A: They look for it together.
        B: They look at night in trees.
        C: They look for fruit with leaves on it.
        D: They look for it alone.

2. (   ) What time might chimps look for food?
        A: 2:00 a.m.   B: 11:00 a.m.
        C: 8:00 p.m.   D: 11:00 p.m.

3. (   ) Chimps are smart. So, _____.
        A: they sleep in trees.
        B: they can solve problems.
        C: they live in groups.
        D: they like to eat.

4. (   ) Which of these is true about chimps?
        A: There may be 800 chimps in a group.
        B: They only live in zoos.
        C: Some groups have fewer than 10 animals.
        D: They like to make fruits and leaves.

Grammar

Combine the two sentences into one sentence.

1. Chimps are smart. Monkeys are smart.

   _____

2. They eat fruit. They eat leaves.

   _____

3. They live in a group. They sleep in trees.

   _____

What to do in New York: May 12-18

Shows

Chicago
Tickets: $25-$125
Time: Daily, 8:00 PM

Phantom of the Opera
Tickets: $15-$75
Time: Mon, Wed, 7:30 PM

Music

Jazz
Location: The Music Well
Time: Starts at 6:00 PM

Rock
Location: Rock the Clock
Time: Starts at 8:00 PM

Museums

Museum of Modern Art
Special showing: French art
Open: 10:00 AM - 6:00 PM

Metropolitan Museum
Special showing: Glass art
Open: 10:00 AM - 6:00 PM

Free Events

Music in the park
Location: Central Park
Date: May 17, all day

Walking tour of New York
Location: Starts at Lincoln Center
Time: May 18, 2:00 PM

Vocabulary

Write the correct word in each blank.

time	park	museum	special	date

1. What's your favorite painting in this _____?

2. The _____ of the party is January 15th.

3. This is a _____ kind of cake. You can only buy it here.

4. What _____ tonight does the movie start?

Choose the best answer.

1. (   ) _____ does not have a music event.
    A: The Metropolitan Museum B: Rock the Clock
    C: Central Park   D: The Music Well

2. (   ) Every section gives _____ the events.
    A: directions to   B: the price of
    C: the time of   D: the size of

3. (   ) Which of these is **not** possible on the same day?
    A: Seeing glass art and watching Phantom of the Opera.
    B: Seeing French art and listening to jazz music.
    C: Seeing French art and glass art.
    D: Seeing Chicago and listening to rock music.

4. (   ) May 12 is a Monday. What could be someone's schedule?

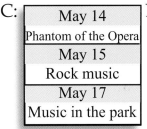

A:		B:		C:		D:	
May 12		May 13		May 14		May 16	
Chicago		Phantom of the Opera		Phantom of the Opera		Music in the park	
May 14		May 14		May 15		May 17	
French art		Jazz music		Rock music		Walking tour	
May 18		May 15		May 17		May 18	
Music in the park		Glass art		Music in the park		French art	

Put the words in the correct order.

1. will cold Wednesday It be on

    _____.

2. at you Will 2:30 me meet

    _____?

3. on Tuesday the museum not will I go to

    _____.

4. at 8:30 will opera The begin

    _____.

Roger: Tell me about fire fighting.

Mr. Black: Well, it's very hot! It can be dangerous, so you need a lot of training.

Roger: Is fighting fires your only job?

Mr. Black: Actually, no. We also help in medical emergencies.

Roger: Why do you like being a firefighter?

Mr. Black: It's something I enjoy. Sure, it's hard. But I like helping people. It gives me a good feeling.

Vocabulary

Write the correct word in each blank.

| something | hot | feeling | enjoy | hard |

1. It's so _____! Let's get some ice cream.

2. Do you _____ living in this city?

3. I need to tell you _____ important. Come here.

4. What's your _____ about this group? Do you like them?

Choose the best answer.

1. (   ) What is the purpose of the conversation?
      A: To train people to do a job.
      B: To find out how to fight fires.
      C: To understand how dangerous fire is.
      D: To learn about a firefighter's work.

2. (   ) Besides fighting fires, Mr. Black sometimes _____.
      A: teaches   B: catches thieves
      C: interviews people   D: helps injured people

3. (   ) What does Mr. Black suggest?
      A: Firefighters earn a lot of money.
      B: Firefighters have to be careful.
      C: Firefighters are afraid of hot weather.
      D: Firefighters are never safe.

4. (   ) Which of these is true?
      A: A firefighter's training is easy.
      B: Mr. Black doesn't like his job.
      C: A firefighter does more than fight fires.
      D: Roger wants to become a firefighter.

Grammar

Match each question with the correct response.

1. __ Where do you work?	A. At a bank.
2. __ How many hours a week do you work?	B. I meet a lot of people.
3. __ What do you like about your job?	C. Sometimes I have to work on the weekend.
4. __ What don't you like about your job?	D. About 40.

19 This Old Car

My car is more than 15 years old. It's not fast. And it's not very nice to look at.

But you know, I really love this car. It runs well, and I take good care of it. I treat it like an old friend. This old car and I have a long history together.

Vocabulary

Write the correct word in each blank.

together	fast	car	treat	love

1. Why do you _____ your dog badly? You should be nice to it.

2. The mall is across the city. We can take my _____.

3. Laura and her best friend go everywhere _____.

4. This train is _____. It only takes 20 minutes.

Choose the best answer.

1. (   ) What is the car like?
   - A: Fast but ugly.
   - B: Nice looking but old.
   - C: Slow but bad.
   - D: Old but good.

2. (   ) How does the person feel about his car?
   - A: He wants a new one.
   - B: He wants to keep it.
   - C: He wants to fix it.
   - D: He wants to give it away.

3. (   ) Why does the old car still run well?
   - A: The man treats it well.
   - B: It's better than all the new cars.
   - C: It likes the man.
   - D: The man drives it quickly.

4. (   ) Which of these is like the man and his car?
   - A: A woman living in an old house for many years.
   - B: Two people at a company.
   - C: A doctor and a nurse working together.
   - D: A man and a new airplane.

Grammar

Put the words in the correct order.

1. car runs old My well

   _____.

2. this car very I well treat old

   _____.

3. is a good It friend very

   _____.

39

20 Cinco de Mayo

Cinco de Mayo (meaning "May 5th" in Spanish) is an important Mexican holiday. On that day, Mexicans remember defeating the French army 150 years ago. It makes Mexicans proud of their country.

There are big parties every May 5th. Friends and relatives eat together. There are parades and concerts. Besides the fun, the holiday brings people closer together.

Vocabulary

Write the correct word in each blank.

remember	proud	holiday	important	party

1. Your son is the winner! You must be _____ of him.

2. What's her phone number? I don't _____ it.

3. Do you want to come to my birthday _____?

4. New Year's Day is a great _____. We don't have to go to work!

Reading

Choose the best answer.

1. (   ) Cinco de Mayo makes Mexicans feel _____ about their country.
   - A: bad
   - B: worried
   - C: good
   - D: sad

2. (   ) Cinco de Mayo is about a day from Mexico's _____.
   - A: land
   - B: past
   - C: future
   - D: party

3. (   ) What is probably true about defeating the French army?
   - A: It's important to Mexicans.
   - B: It's a small event from Mexico's history.
   - C: Only a few people know about it.
   - D: People are trying to forget it.

4. (   ) Which of these is **not** part of the holiday?
   - A: Food
   - B: Music
   - C: Gifts
   - D: Parades

Grammar

Put the words in the correct order.

1. a holiday May Is in there

   _____?

2. aren't August in There holidays any

   _____.

3. city the parade is There a in

   _____.

4. many there Are parties Mexico in

   _____?

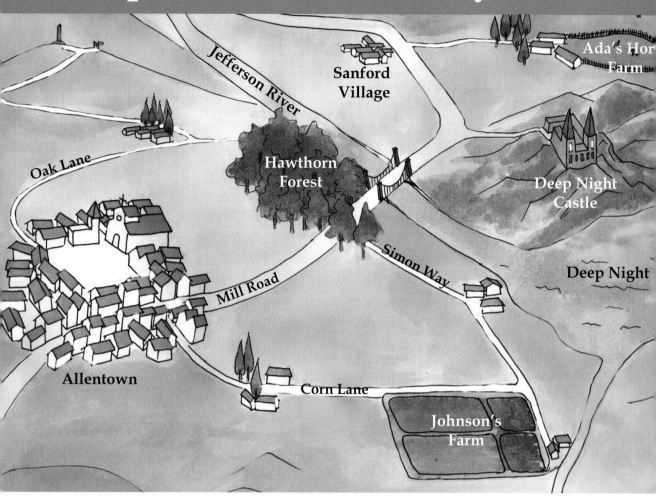

Jefferson River

Oak Lane

Sanford Village

Ada's Hor Farm

Hawthorn Forest

Deep Night Castle

Simon Way

Deep Night

Mill Road

Allentown

Corn Lane

Johnson's Farm

Vocabulary

Write the correct word in each blank.

forest	corn	road	river	village

1. About 200 people live in the _____.

2. A _____ is full of trees.

3. People drive very fast on this _____.

4. The water in this _____ moves very fast.

Reading

Choose the best answer.

1. (   ) Which is closest to Ada's Horse Farm?
- A: Johnson's Farm.
- B: Deep Night Lake.
- C: Allentown.
- D: Deep Night Castle.

2. (   ) Where is Hawthorn Forest?
- A: Across the river from Allentown.
- B: Behind Johnson's Farm.
- C: Along Jefferson River.
- D: Next to Ada's Horse Farm.

3. (   ) Which road does **not** go to Allentown?
- A: Simon Way.   B: Corn Lane.
- C: Oak Lane.   D: Mill Road.

4. (   ) To go from Allentown to Deep Night Castle, _____.
- A: you have to pass Johnson's Farm
- B: you have to cross a bridge
- C: you do not go by Hawthorn Forest
- D: you have to go down Simon Way

Grammar

Complete each sentence with *to, in, at,* or *on.*

1. The castle sits _____ a hill.

2. Simon Way begins _____ the forest.

3. Corn Lane meets Simon Way _____ the farm.

4. Mill Road goes _____ Sanford Village.

22 A Computer Expert

Casey knows a lot about computers. He can put them together. He can also fix them. Friends ask for his help with computer problems.

Casey reads books to teach himself more. He also spends a lot of time on the Internet. What does Casey do for fun? That's right – he plays computer games!

Vocabulary

Write the correct word in each blank.

about	fix	spend	game	teach

1. Can you _____ me to play the piano?

2. My TV isn't working. Can you _____ it?

3. Tell me more _____ your country.

4. We need four people to play this _____.

Choose the best answer.

1. (　) What is the purpose of the story?
　　　A: To introduce a person.
　　　B: To teach people about computers.
　　　C: To talk about a problem.
　　　D: To tell people about the Internet.

2. (　) How does Casey learn more about computers?
　　　A: He teaches himself with books.
　　　B: He takes classes.
　　　C: He asks friends for help.
　　　D: He puts computers together.

3. (　) Casey does **not** _____ computers.
　　　A: fix　　　　　　　　B: sell
　　　C: build　　　　　　　D: study

4. (　) What might Casey say?
　　　A: "Watching TV is my favorite thing to do."
　　　B: "Computers are a lot of fun."
　　　C: "Reading isn't very useful."
　　　D: "My friends can all fix computers."

Grammar

Put the words in the correct order.

1. he computer Can my fix

_____?

2. you help me Can this problem with

_____?

3. can't this computer together put I

_____.

4. You ask for help him can

_____.

23 Thank You Note

Thank you!

Dear Marie,

Thank you very much for the vase. I really love it!
I have the perfect spot for it. In my living room,
there's a small table. That's the vase's new home!

Now I need to go to the flower store. I'm thinking
of roses or daisies...

Anyway, thank you again!

Angela

Thank you!

Vocabulary

Write the correct word in each blank.

perfect	store	need	living room	really

1. It's too dark in here. We _____ more light.

2. Is there a clothing _____ near here? I want to buy some socks.

3. Many people have a TV and sofa in their _____.

4. That's a _____ good idea. I should write it down.

Choose the best answer.

1. (   ) Angela _____.
    A: really likes the present
    B: doesn't have any feeling about the present
    C: thinks the present is perfect
    D: hates the present

2. (   ) What do we know about Angela's living room?
    A: It has a new table.
    B: There's a place for the vase.
    C: It's full of different things.
    D: There are a lot of flowers in it.

3. (   ) What does "spot" mean in the first paragraph?
    A: table   B: place
    C: vase   D: house

4. (   ) Why does Angela want to go to a store?
    A: To buy a vase.   B: To buy some flowers.
    C: To buy a table.   D: To buy something for Marie.

Grammar

Match each sentence with the correct answer.

1. __ Thank you very much!

2. __ You don't have to buy me a present.

3. __ What do you want for your birthday?

4. __ Do you like your present?

A. Some DVDs.

B. Of course! I love it!

C. You're welcome.

D. I know. But I want to.

Vocabulary

Write the correct word in each blank.

class	fine	interesting	English	student

1. Gary is a good _____. He studies very hard.

2. I feel _____. I'm not sick anymore.

3. I use _____ every day on the Internet.

4. Science _____ is hard. We have so much homework!

Choose the best answer.

1. (   )   A: How are you?
            B: Where are you from?
            C: I like our history class.
            D: Nice to meet you.

2. (   )   A: you are
            B: he is
            C: we are
            D: I am

3. (   )   A: that's no problem
            B: that must be hard
            C: lucky you
            D: I don't speak English either

4. (   )   A: everyone
            B: nothing
            C: anything
            D: any time

Grammar

Match each question with the correct answer.

1. __ How are you?   **A.** Yes, thank you.

2. __ What are you doing?   **B.** I'm doing well, thanks.

3. __ Do you need any help?   **C.** I'm from Canada.

4. __ Where are you from?   **D.** I'm watching TV.

25 Space Dreams

Linus has big dreams. He doesn't want a normal job in a tall building. Linus wants to work much higher up – in space.

Linus could work in a space station. Or he might fly a space ship. He could even travel to Mars. Day and night, Linus dreams with stars in his eyes.

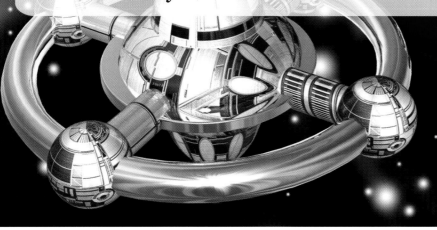

Vocabulary

Write the correct word in each blank.

building	space	normal	work	fly

1. We plan to _____ from here to England.

2. My office is in that _____ over there.

3. This is _____ weather for May.

4. Do you ever look up at the stars in _____?

Choose the best answer.

1. ( ) When does Linus think about space?
   A: All the time.   B: During the day.
   C: At night, in his dreams.   D: At work.

2. ( ) Which space job is **not** in the story?
   A: Flying a space ship.
   B: Traveling to another planet.
   C: Building tall buildings on the moon.
   D: Doing a job on a space station.

3. ( ) Which of these might Linus want to be?
   A: B: C: D:

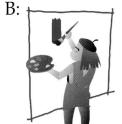

4. ( ) What would Linus say about a job at a bank?
   A: "That sounds great!"
   B: "That's my dream job!"
   C: "I can make a lot of money there."
   D: "It's not for me."

Grammar

Complete each sentence with *might, could,* or *can't.*

1. I _____ go with you. I don't have any money.

2. Excuse me, Peter. _____ I speak with you?

3. Sorry, we _____ go out. We have to stay home.

4. I _____ not go to work today. I don't feel well.

26 The Iditarod

The Iditarod is a dogsled race across Alaska. Every March, around 65 teams take part. Each team has one person and up to 16 dogs.

Together, they race almost 2000 kilometers. It's a long, hard, and very cold race. Just finishing the Iditarod is not easy. Winning it is a dream come true!

Vocabulary   Write the correct word in each blank.

almost	cold	dream	easy	across

1. My _____ is to open my own pet shop.

2. The car is _____ full. There's room for one more box.

3. Ted's job is _____. He only works three hours a day.

4. Katie, my best friend, lives _____ the street. I see her every day.

Choose the best answer.

1. (   ) About how many teams race in the Iditarod?
        A: 16.
        B: 17.
        C: 65.
        D: 2000.

2. (   ) The article does **not** say the race is _____.
        A: long   B: hard
        C: short   D: cold

3. (   ) "Winning it is a dream come true." What does this mean?
        A: You have to dream to win.
        B: Everything in life is hard to get.
        C: People think about winning the race for a long time.
        D: People dream a lot at night.

4. (   ) What does the article suggest about the Iditarod?
        A: All the teams easily finish the race.
        B: Every team has a good chance of winning.
        C: Teams have to work hard just to finish.
        D: Teams only win in their dreams.

Grammar

Complete each sentence with *I, me,* or *my.*

1. My dog and _____ are good friends.

2. _____ team won the race.

3. It was not easy for _____ to do that.

4. Winning the game was _____ biggest dream.

Candy and soda are "junk food." They sometimes taste good, but they are bad for you.

Junk food like candy and soda is full of sugar. Eating a lot of sugar is not healthy. It can even make you sick. It's better to eat healthy food. Fruits and vegetables are two kinds of good food.

Vocabulary

Write the correct word in each blank.

taste	kind	sick	candy	healthy

1. You look _____. You should see a doctor.

2. What _____ of dog is that?

3. It's almost dinner time. Don't eat any more _____.

4. _____ this soup. Is it good?

Reading

Choose the best answer.

1. (   ) What is bad about junk food?
   - A: It has a lot of sugar.
   - B: It tastes good.
   - C: It's natural.
   - D: It's like fruits and vegetables.

2. (   ) Soda is an example of _____.
   - A: a fruit
   - B: a healthy food
   - C: a kind of junk food
   - D: something without a lot of sugar

3. (   ) What is "it" in the second paragraph?
   - A: Eating.
   - B: Eating a lot of sugar.
   - C: Junk food.
   - D: Healthy food.

4. (   ) What does the article suggest about vegetables?
   - A: They have a lot of sugar.
   - B: They don't taste good.
   - C: They're the same as junk food.
   - D: They're good for you.

Grammar

Combine the two sentences into one with *and* or *but.*

1. Candy is sweet. It's not good for you.

   _____.

2. It tastes good. It's bad for you.

   _____.

3. Apples taste good. They are good for you.

   _____.

28 Movie Posters

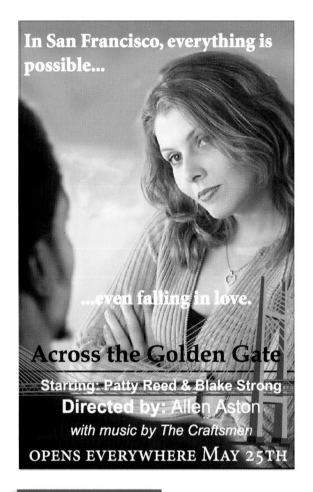

In San Francisco, everything is possible...

...even falling in love.

Across the Golden Gate

Starring: Patty Reed & Blake Strong
Directed by: Allen Aston
with music by The Craftsmen
OPENS EVERYWHERE MAY 25TH

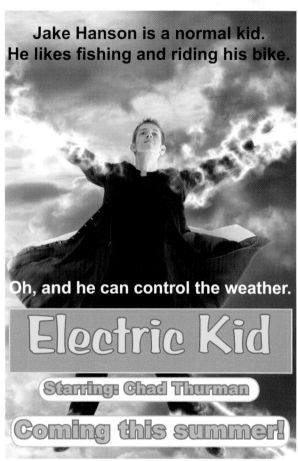

Jake Hanson is a normal kid.
He likes fishing and riding his bike.

Oh, and he can control the weather.

Electric Kid

Starring: Chad Thurman

Coming this summer!

Vocabulary

Write the correct word in each blank.

control	bike	everything	ride	possible

1. Bring _____ with you. Don't leave anything here.

2. On farms, people still _____ horses.

3. Sure, I want to open a big company. But is it really _____?

4. It's raining hard. I don't want to ride my _____ to work.

Choose the best answer.

1. (   ) When might *Electric Kid* open?
>   A: In January
>   B: In April.
>   C: In July.
>   D: In October.

2. (   ) What is something both posters show?
>   A: The movie's opening date.
>   B: The name(s) of the music writer(s).
>   C: The name(s) of the starring actor(s).
>   D: The director's name.

3. (   ) The poster does **not** say the Electric Kid _____.
>   A: can control the weather   B: lives in San Francisco
>   C: likes to fish   D: enjoys bike riding

4. (   ) What kind of movie is *Across the Golden Gate*?
>   A: Funny.
>   B: Scary.
>   C: Sad.
>   D: Romantic.

Grammar

Write the correct form of the word.

1. The new movie is _____ (open) soon.

2. It is _____ (come) this summer.

3. It _____ (be) starring Antonio Banderos.

4. They _____ (be) falling in love.

29 What do you think?

What do you think about sports?

 **Jessica:** I love sports. I play softball with my friends on Fridays.

 **Chun Kyu:** I don't play any sports. But I like to watch them on TV.

 **Carlos:** I play sports to have fun. I don't care about winning.

 **Abdul:** Actually, I'm not interested in sports. I don't like them or hate them.

Vocabulary

Write the correct word in each blank.

sport	friend	watch	fun	win

1. Let's _____ the game on TV.

2. This is my good _____, John.

3. Basketball is my favorite _____. I play every week.

4. Try hard! We can still _____ the game!

58

Reading

Choose the best answer.

1. (   ) What is the purpose of the reading?
      A: To find out how to win at sports.
      B: To learn what sports are popular in each country.
      C: To hear people's opinions about sports.
      D: To tell people everything about sports.

2. (   ) What do we learn about these people?
      A: They don't understand the question.
      B: They have different ideas about sports.
      C: None of them play any sports.
      D: They have the same ideas about sports.

3. (   ) On the weekend, Chun Kyu might _____.
      A: play softball   B: watch basketball on TV
      C: win a new TV   D: watch a game with Abdul

4. (   ) What is important to Carlos?
      A: Having a good time. B: Winning a lot of money.
      C: Being the best.   D: Making new friends.

Grammar

Write the correct form of the word.

1. I _____ (do n't) like sports.

2. She _____ (do n't) play softball.

3. We _____ (do n't) care about winning.

4. It _____ (be n't) a lot of fun.

30 Hurricanes

A hurricane is a strong storm. It starts over the ocean. Its wind goes around and around. Slowly, it moves across the ocean.

Hurricanes often move across land. They bring strong wind (up to 150 miles per hour). They also bring heavy rain (sometimes many inches). In this dangerous weather, people have to be careful.

Vocabulary Write the correct word in each blank.

dangerous	strong	weather	starts	wind

1. The party _____ at 7:30.

2. Don't walk in the street. It's _____.

3. I love sunny _____. It makes me happy.

4. I think you are very _____. Can you open this bottle?

Choose the best answer.

1. (   ) Where does a hurricane start?
    A: Near land.   B: Over land.
    C: In the ocean.   D: Over the ocean.

2. (   ) A hurricane is a _____ storm.
    A: cold   B: dangerous
    C: dry   D: safe

3. (   ) What happens last?
    A: A hurricane goes around and around.
    B: A hurricane brings strong winds to a country.
    C: A hurricane starts over the ocean.
    D: A hurricane moves across the ocean.

4. (   ) Which of these is true?
    A: Hurricanes often bring 150 meters of rain.
    B: The wind moves in a circle.
    C: Hurricanes always pass over land.
    D: The wind can move a few kilometers per hour.

Grammar

Combine the two sentences into one sentence.

1. It is a storm. The storm is big.

   _____

2. Rain is falling across the land. The rain is heavy.

   _____

3. I don't like this weather. It is dangerous.

   _____

31 Being a Good Language Learner

Learning a new language is not easy. Do you want to be a better learner? Here are a few ways:

- **Pay attention in class. (Listen to the teacher.)**
- **Work hard in class. (Speak out a lot.)**
- **Do your homework. (Exercises are very important.)**
- **Practice more. (For example, keep a journal or write stories.)**

Vocabulary

Write the correct word or words in each blank.

for example	way	homework	practice

1. You play the violin so well! Do you _____ a lot?

2. What's a good _____ to exercise?

3. I spend an hour a day on my science _____.

4. Mr. Park is a good teacher. _____, he listens to us.

Choose the best answer.

1. (   ) The reading says learning a new language is _____.
      A: easy   B: important
      C: hard   D: great

2. (   ) How can you work hard in class?
      A: Talk a lot.
      B: Pay attention to classmates.
      C: Write cards for friends.
      D: Do your homework in class.

3. (   ) Which of these is **not** suggested?
      A: Doing nothing in class.
      B: Doing exercises.
      C: Doing extra writing practice.
      D: Doing homework.

4. (   ) Which of these is true?
      A: Writing isn't important.
      B: There's only one way to be a better learner.
      C: The article gives more than one idea.
      D: You should do your classmates' homework.

Grammar

Put the words in the correct order.

1. new language is Learning not a easy

   _____.

2. attention in class Paying is important

   _____.

3. journal keeping Is a helpful

   _____?

4. out Speaking writing and important are

   _____.

32 The Knowledge

London, England, is a big city. Becoming a taxi driver is hard. First, people take a course: "The Knowledge."

Finishing The Knowledge takes several years. You study 400 different routes. You learn about London's famous places. Then, you must pass several tests. Finally, you can be a London taxi driver.

Vocabulary

Write the correct word in each blank.

finish	year	different	become	several

1. There are _____ apples left. Have one.

2. Do you want to _____ rich? Then you must work hard!

3. I want to travel to India next _____.

4. That's not my purse. Mine is a _____ color.

Choose the best answer.

1. (   ) What is The Knowledge?
   - A: A course of study.
   - B: A place in London.
   - C: A famous school.
   - D: A test.

2. (   ) To become a London taxi driver, you do **not** _____.
   - A: learn 400 routes in the city
   - B: take tests
   - C: study famous places
   - D: teach people about The Knowledge

3. (   ) What comes last?
   - A: Passing a test.
   - B: Studying routes.
   - C: Becoming a taxi driver.
   - D: Learning The Knowledge.

4. (   ) Which of these is true?
   - A: Drivers can pay money to pass The Knowledge.
   - B: Drivers learn about 400 famous places.
   - C: There are 400 taxi drivers in London.
   - D: Finishing The Knowledge takes more than one year.

Grammar   Complete each sentence with *first, then,* or *finally.*

Sundays are busy days for me. _____, I read my email.

That's in the morning. _____, I take a taxi to a restaurant.

I have lunch with some friends. _____, I take my dog for

a walk. _____, I clean my house. I work really hard

on the weekend!

33 My Mother

My mother is a great person. When I ___(1)___ a child, she ___(2)___ me stories. She listened to my problems. She ___(3)___ my world a better place.

Besides all that, she worked at her office, and she _(4)_ the house clean. Now, today she is still a great cook and my great friend.

Vocabulary

Write the correct word in each blank.

listen	clean	house	cook	story

1. I want to _____ dinner tonight.

2. My room is never _____. I can't find anything in there!

3. There are four rooms in my _____.

4. _____ to your father. He's a smart man.

Choose the best answer.

1. (　)　A: being
　　　　B: is
　　　　C: was
　　　　D: were

2. (　)　A: tells
　　　　B: told
　　　　C: telling
　　　　D: tell

3. (　)　A: make
　　　　B: made
　　　　C: making
　　　　D: makes

4. (　)　A: keeps
　　　　B: keeping
　　　　C: kept
　　　　D: keep

Grammar

Write the correct form of the word.

When I worked for that company, it _____ (was/were) a great place. All of us _____ (was/were) good friends. My best friend _____ (was/were) Nell. We _____ (was/were) very happy there. Now it is not a good place to work.

Recipe #23

Chocolate Chip Cookies

Ingredients:

2 cups of chocolate chips
1 teaspoon of baking soda
1 teaspoon of vanilla
2 1/2 cups of flour   2 eggs
3/4 cup of white sugar   1 teaspoon of salt
1 cup of brown sugar   1 cup of butter

Directions:

1) Preheat the oven to 375 degrees F.
   (190 degrees C)
2) Use a large bowl to mix the butter, white sugar, and brown sugar.
3) Mix in the eggs, one at a time. Stir in the vanilla.
4) In a small bowl, mix the salt, baking soda, and flour. Add the mix to the large bowl.
5) Add the chocolate chips to the large bowl.
6) Put spoonfuls of the mix onto a baking pan.
7) Bake for 10 minutes.

Vocabulary

Write the correct word in each blank.

minutes	bowl	large	sugar	mix

1. We live in a _____ city. It has five million people.

2. Should I _____ the water and flour together?

3. I like _____ and milk in my coffee.

4. The dog is thirsty. Put more water in its _____.

Choose the best answer.

1. (   ) How many steps are in the directions?

     A: 1.   B: 7.

     C: 12.   D: 23.

2. (   ) You mix the butter and sugar _____.

     A: in the oven

     B: in the small bowl

     C: in the big bowl

     D: in the baking pan

3. (   ) What does "one at a time" mean?

     A: one after another

     B: one each day

     C: one before the first one

     D: one second

4. (   ) What is **not** on the recipe card?

     A: A picture of the food.

     B: The number of the recipe.

     C: The list of ingredients.

     D: The date of the recipe.

Grammar

Put the words in the correct order.

1. some   cookies   made   I

   _____.

2. ingredients   all   mixed   I   First   the

   _____.

3. chips   chocolate   Then   I   added

   _____.

4. for   minutes   10   I   baked   Finally   them

   _____.

Ron: How is your Christmas shopping going?

Salina: So-so. I need to buy something for my brother, Miguel. He's 10. He wants computer games.

Karen: So does mine. (He's 16.) But I want to get him some clothes.

Dan: How boring! Who wants clothes for Christmas?

Salina: I do.

Dan: That's you. You're 15.

Salina: So? Karen's 14. She wants clothes, too.

Karen: Right! And some makeup.

Vocabulary

Write the correct word in each blank.

| clothes | want | boring | brother | shopping |

1. I have two sisters and one _____.

2. Many people _____ to make a lot of money.

3. Let's go _____ at the new mall.

4. This city is never _____. There's so much to do!

Choose the best answer.

1. (   ) Who wants clothes for Christmas?
   A: Dan and Karen's brother.
   B: Ron and Dan.
   C: Salina and Karen.
   D: Karen and Miguel.

2. (   ) Who is the oldest person?
   A: Salina.   B: Salina's brother.
   C: Karen.   D: Karen's brother.

3. (   ) What might Salina like for Christmas?
   A: A video game.
   B: A dress.
   C: Lipstick.
   D: The same thing as Dan.

4. (   ) What might Dan say to Salina?
   A: "You're young. So, you want makeup."
   B: "You and your brother want the same thing."
   C: "Your brother is older. So, he wants clothes."
   D: "You're not so young. So, you want some clothes."

Grammar

Complete each sentence with *I, me, my,* or *mine.*

1. Miguel is _____ brother.

2. _____ gave him a computer game.

3. My brother gave _____ clothes.

4. _____ did, too.

36 Skateboarding

Skateboarding is a lot of fun. All you need is a skateboard. Skaters sometimes fall off their boards. So it's smart to wear pads and a helmet, too.

There are special parks for riding skateboards. They have ramps and jumps. And skaters don't have to worry about cars or other dangers.

Vocabulary

Write the correct word in each blank.

fall off	wear	danger	worry	their

1. It's cold. You should _____ a jacket.

2. You shouldn't ride your motorcycle so fast! You might _____.

3. I love visiting my aunt and uncle. _____ house is so big.

4. Don't _____. This area is very safe.

Choose the best answer.

1. (   ) For skateboarding, it's best to have _____.
    A: a lot of money   B: a park in your house
    C: a board and safety items   D: just a skateboard

2. (   ) Why should skaters wear a helmet?
    A: It looks cool.
    B: Skaters sometimes fall down.
    C: Skateboarding is safe.
    D: Pads are too expensive.

3. (   ) Where is the safest place to ride?
    A: Skateboard parks.
    B: City streets.
    C: All city parks.
    D: Near your house.

4. (   ) What does the article suggest about cars?
    A: They can be dangerous to skaters.
    B: There are too many of them.
    C: They are not safe to drive.
    D: They try to hit skaters.

Grammar

Complete each sentence with *there was* or *there were*.

1. _____ a lot of skates there.

2. It snowed. _____ so much snow on the ground!

3. _____ too many people in the skateboard park.

4. We didn't run. _____ a lot of time left.

Saturday Is My Day!

Staying up late on Friday,
Waking up late the next day,
Spending time in my own way,
Saturday is my day!

Listening to my CDs,
Watching some old DVDs,
Finding good shows on TV,
Saturday is just for me!

Going out or staying indoors,
Shopping at my favorite store,
Seeing friends a little more,
Saturday is great, for sure!

Vocabulary

Write the correct word in each blank.

favorite	just	wake up	find	next

1. What's your _____ kind of ice cream?

2. I can't go anywhere this week. How about _____ week?

3. I usually _____ at 8:00.

4. This ride is _____ for children. You can't go on it.

Reading

Choose the best answer.

1. (   ) How does the writer feel about Saturday?
   A: Bored.   B: Tired.
   C: Excited.   D: Lonely.

2. (   ) What does the writer do on Friday?
   A: He or she wakes up late.
   B: He or she sees friends.
   C: He or she goes to the movies.
   D: He or she goes to sleep late.

3. (   ) This poem has three parts (called stanzas). Which stanza
   is about music and movies?
   A: The first stanza.   B: The second stanza.
   C: The third stanza.   D: None of the stanzas.

4. (   ) The writer does **not** write about _____.
   A: cleaning the house   B: buying things
   C: staying home   D: watching TV

Grammar

Complete each sentence with *am, are,* or *is.*

1. I _____ going to stay up late.

2. She _____ going to wake up late.

3. _____ we going to watch TV?

4. They _____ not going to stay indoors.

75

38 The Calgary Stampede

The Calgary Stampede is a big event in Canada. Every July, more than one million people attend.

At the Stampede, there is a big rodeo. Riders show their horse and bull riding skills.

There are also farm animal shows, art shows, and more. What an event! Canadians call it "The Greatest Outdoor Show on Earth."

Vocabulary

Write the correct word in each blank.

horse	call	farm	skill	show

1. They grow corn and potatoes on their _____.

2. This tastes great! What do you _____ it?

3. You should _____ me your house some day.

4. Flying an airplane takes a lot of _____.

Choose the best answer.

1. (   ) About how many people attend the Stampede?
   - A: 1,000.
   - B: 100,000.
   - C: 1,000,000.
   - D: 10,000,000.

2. (   ) What happens at a rodeo?
   - A: People sell animals.
   - B: People ride horses and bulls.
   - C: People make art.
   - D: People visit Canada.

3. (   ) The article does **not** have information about _____.
   - A: the month of the Stampede
   - B: the Stampede's country
   - C: the Stampede's events
   - D: the cost to attend the Stampede

4. (   ) Which of these does the Stampede have?
   - A: Rodeos with one million horses.
   - B: Shows with animals in them.
   - C: Free bull riding classes.
   - D: Bull races.

Grammar
Put the words in the correct order.

1. year Last attended the we Calgary Stampede

   _____.

2. very skillful were The riders

   _____.

3. great The shows animal were

   _____.

4. there lots of events Were

   _____?

39 MP3 Players

Many people listen to music on MP3 players. They are small and cheap. You can carry them anywhere.

You transfer songs from a computer to the player. MP3 players can hold many songs. Some even hold thousands of songs, and the battery usually lasts a long time.

Vocabulary

Write the correct word in each blank.

anywhere	song	computer	cheap	carry

1. Is the food in this restaurant _____? I don't have a lot of money.

2. Help me _____ these boxes. The car's over there.

3. We can go _____. We don't need to stay here.

4. My _____ doesn't work. I can't go onto the Internet.

Choose the best answer.

1. (   ) What are MP3 players like?
        A: They're large and nice.
        B: They're cheap and popular.
        C: They're expensive and interesting.
        D: They're hard and fun.

2. (   ) You use a(n) _____ to get songs onto a player.
        A: battery   B: radio
        C: MP3   D: computer

3. (   ) What may be true about the battery?
        A: It may last only a few minutes.
        B: It may be the worst thing about the player.
        C: It may cost you a lot of money.
        D: It may last many hours.

4. (   ) Which of these points is **not** in the article?
        A: The price of MP3 players.
        B: The color of MP3 players.
        C: The size of MP3 players.
        D: The battery of MP3 players.

Grammar

Write the correct word in each blank.

1. We can eat _____. Why do you want to eat here?
      (anywhere/somewhere)

2. There's _____ outside your house!
      (anyone/someone)

3. I don't know _____ here.
      (anybody/somebody)

4. Does _____ have a battery?
      (anybody/somebody)

40 Oil

Think about a world without oil. We need it for so many things. Machines need oil to run. Gas (for cars) comes from oil. We also use oil to make many things.

However, our oil supply is low, and the price is going up. These are big problems. We need to solve them

Vocabulary

Write the correct word in each blank.

solve	price	without	machine	use

1. I _____ a computer at work.

2. This _____ puts the fruit into cans.

3. People can't live _____ water.

4. The _____ is too high. I can't buy it.

Choose the best answer.

1. (   ) What can we say about oil?
   A: It is very useful.
   B: It is cheap.
   C: It is not important.
   D: It is not from this world.

2. (   ) Which of these do **not** use oil?
   A: Machines.   B: Cars.
   C: Prices.   D: Factories.

3. (   ) What does the article suggest?
   A: There is a lot of oil left.
   B: Oil is only a little useful.
   C: The high price of oil is a problem.
   D: We have plenty of time to solve our problems.

4. (   ) Which of these is **not** true?
   A: Gas comes from oil.
   B: Machines need oil.
   C: There is still a big supply of oil.
   D: Oil is not cheap.

Grammar

Put the words in the correct order.

1. solve We this problem need to

   _____.

2. we need Do to use oil

   _____?

3. oil so much We need don't use to

   _____.

4. want about this think to I

   _____.

Answer Key

Unit 1

Vocabulary
1. many
2. also
3. long
4. secret

Reading
1. B   2. A
3. D   4. B

Grammar
1. South America is not a country.
2. Are there many fish in the river?
3. It is the world's biggest country.

Unit 2

Vocabulary
1. winter
2. smells
3. inside
4. often

Reading
1. B   2. A
3. A   4. B

Grammar
1. She spends time outside in the fall.
2. We swim in the summer.
3. I like to eat ice cream.
4. The spring flowers smell great.

Unit 3

Vocabulary
1. friendly
2. play
3. around
4. music

Reading
1. A   2. B
3. A   4. B

Grammar
1. his
2. He
3. him
4. his

Unit 4

Vocabulary
1. look for
2. other
3. library
4. walk

Reading
1. D   2. A
3. C   4. B

Grammar
1. is
2. Am
3. are
4. Is

Unit 5

Vocabulary
1. a few
2. movie
3. eat
4. plain

Reading
1. C   2. A
3. B   4. D

Grammar
1. Is it easy to make?
2. People eat it at the movies.
3. It is a very popular snack.
4. It's fun to eat at home.

Unit 6

Vocabulary
1. anyone
2. agree
3. laugh
4. polite

Reading
1. C   2. A
3. D   4. B

Grammar
1. are
2. are
3. is
4. am

Unit 7

Vocabulary
1. snow
2. cloudy
3. painting
4. hide

Reading
1. B   2. D
3. C   4. C

Grammar
1. The mountain is covered with snow.
2. It isn't very cloudy today.
3. Are there many poems about Fuji?
4. Is she an old friend?

Unit 8

Vocabulary
1. age
2. total
3. water
4. Spring

Reading
1. D   2. D
3. B   4. B

Grammar
1. Why
2. How much
3. When
4. What

Unit 9

Vocabulary
1. Internet
2. careful
3. read
4. school

Reading
1. C   2. B
3. D   4. A

Grammar
1. C   2. D
3. B   4. A

Unit 10

Vocabulary
1. get
2. help
3. right
4. ticket

Reading
1. A   2. D
3. D   4. C

Grammar
1. Here is your change.
2. Are the tickets twenty dollars?
3. That is not a good deal!

Unit 11

Vocabulary
1. home
2. fish
3. swim
4. beautiful

Reading
1. B 2. A
3. C 4. B

Grammar
1. C 2. A
3. D 4. B

Unit 12

Vocabulary
1. morning
2. expensive
3. phone
4. choose

Reading
1. C 2. B
3. B 4. B

Grammar
1. I like to relax on the weekend.
2. Does it get very cold here at night?
3. She doesn't see friends in the morning.
4. My mother sleeps for an hour in the afternoon.

Unit 13

Vocabulary
1. should
2. glue
3. train
4. build

Reading
1. C 2. B
3. C 4. B

Grammar
1. Let's find a good place to work.
2. Shall we read the instructions now?
3. Let's not use that glue.
4. Let's paint our boat red.

Unit 14

Vocabulary
1. color
2. hour
3. learn
4. artist

Reading
1. C 2. D
3. B 4. A

Grammar
1. Using computers is a lot of fun.
2. Adding color takes a lot of time.
3. Becoming an artist isn't easy.
4. Finishing the work also takes time.

Unit 15

Vocabulary
1. know
2. great
3. soon
4. every

Reading
1. B 2. D
3. C 4. A

Grammar
1. C 2. A
3. B 4. D

Unit 16

Vocabulary
1. group
2. problem
3. live
4. make

Reading
1. A   2. B
3. B   4. C

Grammar
1. Chimps and monkeys are smart.
2. They eat fruit and leaves.
3. They live in a group and sleep in trees.

Unit 17

Vocabulary
1. museum
2. date
3. special
4. time

Reading
1. A   2. C
3. D   4. C

Grammar
1. It will be cold on Wednesday.
2. Will you meet me at 2:30?
3. I will not go to the museum on Tuesday.
4. The opera will begin at 8:30.

Unit 18

Vocabulary
1. hot
2. enjoy
3. something
4. feeling

Reading
1. D   2. D
3. B   4. C

Grammar
1. A   2. D
3. B   4. C

Unit 19

Vocabulary
1. treat
2. car
3. together
4. fast

Reading
1. D   2. B
3. A   4. A

Grammar
1. My old car runs well.
2. I treat this old car very well.
3. It is a very good friend.

Unit 20

Vocabulary
1. proud
2. remember
3. party
4. holiday

Reading
1. C   2. B
3. A   4. C

Grammar
1. Is there a holiday in May?
2. There aren't any holidays in August.
3. There is a parade in the city.
4. Are there many parties in Mexico?

Unit 21

Vocabulary
1. village
2. forest
3. road
4. river

Reading
1. D   2. C
3. A   4. B

Grammar
1. on
2. in
3. at
4. to

Unit 22

Vocabulary
1. teach
2. fix
3. about
4. game

Reading
1. A   2. A
3. B   4. B

Grammar
1. Can he fix my computer?
2. Can you help me with this problem?
3. I can't put this computer together.
4. You can ask him for help.

Unit 23

Vocabulary
1. need
2. store
3. living room
4. really

Reading
1. A   2. B
3. B   4. B

Grammar
1. C   2. D
3. A   4. B

Unit 24

Vocabulary
1. student
2. fine
3. English
4. class

Reading
1. D   2. D
3. B   4. C

Grammar
1. B   2. D
3. A   4. C

Unit 25

Vocabulary
1. fly
2. building
3. normal
4. space

Reading
1. A   2. C
3. C   4. D

Grammar
1. can't
2. Could/Might
3. can't
4. might

Unit 26

Vocabulary
1. dream
2. almost
3. easy
4. across

Reading
1. C   2. C
3. C   4. C

Grammar
1. I
2. My
3. me
4. my

Unit 27

Vocabulary
1. sick
2. kind
3. candy
4. Taste

Reading
1. A   2. C
3. B   4. D

Grammar
1. Candy is sweet, but it's not good for you.
2. It tastes good, but it's bad for you.
3. Apples taste good, and they are good for you.

Unit 28

Vocabulary
1. everything
2. ride
3. possible
4. bike

Reading
1. C   2. C
3. B   4. D

Grammar
1. opening
2. coming
3. is
4. are

Unit 29

Vocabulary
1. watch
2. friend
3. sport
4. win

Reading
1. C   2. B
3. B   4. A

Grammar
1. don't
2. doesn't
3. don't
4. isn't

Unit 30

Vocabulary
1. starts
2. dangerous
3. weather
4. strong

Reading
1. D   2. B
3. B   4. B

Grammar
1. It is a big storm.
2. Heavy rain is falling across the land.
3. I don't like this dangerous weather.

Unit 31

Vocabulary
1. practice
2. way
3. homework
4. for example

Reading
1. C   2. A
3. A   4. C

Grammar
1. Learning a new language is not easy.
2. Paying attention in class is important.
3. Is keeping a journal helpful?
4. Speaking out and writing are important.

Unit 32

Vocabulary
1. several
2. become
3. year
4. different

Reading
1. A   2. D
3. C   4. D

Grammar
1. First
2. Then
3. Then
4. Finally

Unit 33

Vocabulary
1. cook
2. clean
3. house
4. Listen

Reading
1. C   2. B
3. B   4. C

Grammar
1. was
2. were
3. was
4. were

Unit 34

Vocabulary
1. large
2. mix
3. sugar
4. bowl

Reading
1. B   2. C
3. A   4. D

Grammar
1. I made some cookies.
2. First I mixed all the ingredients.
3. Then I added chocolate chips.
4. Finally I baked them for 10 minutes.

Unit 35

Vocabulary
1. brother
2. want
3. shopping
4. boring

Reading
1. C   2. D
3. B   4. D

Grammar
1. my
2. I
3. me
4. Mine

Unit 36

Vocabulary
1. wear
2. fall off
3. Their
4. worry

Reading
1. C   2. B
3. A   4. A

Grammar
1. There were
2. There was
3. There were
4. There was

Unit 37

Vocabulary
1. favorite
2. next
3. wake up
4. just

Reading
1. C   2. D
3. B   4. A

Grammar
1. am   2. is
3. Are   4. are

Unit 38

Vocabulary
1. farm
2. call
3. show
4. skill

Reading
1. C   2. B
3. D   4. B

Grammar
1. Last year we attended the Calgary Stampede.
2. The riders were very skillful.
3. The animal shows were great.
4. Were there lots of events?

Unit 39

Vocabulary
1. cheap
2. carry
3. anywhere
4. computer

Reading
1. B   2. D
3. D   4. B

Grammar
1. anywhere
2. someone
3. anybody
4. anybody

Unit 40

Vocabulary
1. use
2. machine
3. without
4. price

Reading
1. A   2. C
3. C   4. C

Grammar
1. We need to solve this problem.
2. Do we need to use oil?
3. We don't need to use so much oil.
4. I want to think about this.

Series Format

This book is the first in a series of four readers called The Read and Learn Series for beginning-level students. There are 40 units in each book. The readings in this book average about 50 words in length, and a total of just over 600 different words are used in the 40 readings. A summary of the series is below:

Book One: Read 50
   50-Word Reading Passages
   at the 600-word level

Book Two: Read 75
   75-Word Reading Passages
   at the 700-word level

Book Three: Read 100
   100-Word Reading Passages
   at the 800-word level

Book Four: Read 125
   125-Word Reading Passages
   at the 900-word level

The simple and easy-to-use units follow the same two-page format in all four volumes. A reading is followed by three short exercises that correlate with and expand upon the topical and linguistic content in the reading. Answers to the exercises are found at the back of the book.

The content of the units is broad and comprehensive in its appeal and may be used by learners from middle school to community college, and even beyond.

Reading Passages

The readings in the books include a variety of written material: articles, stories, conversations, menus, charts, diagrams, schedules, and Internet pages and messages. The readings are intended to be entertaining, informative, and useful. They focus on the various reading skills required for living and learning in our contemporary English-speaking world. They are international in scope to stimulate interest in and knowledge of other places and cultures, from the Amazon to Mount Fuji, and to emphasize that English is an international language.

Exercises

Following each reading there are **three types of exercises.** The first is a simple multiple choice exercise that focuses on the meaning and use of selected **vocabulary** items from the reading. In general, the items are used in a context that is somewhat different from the context in the reading. The **reading** exercise checks the students' comprehension of the reading. It requires the students to find specific information and to infer additional, more implicit meanings in the text. The **grammar** exercise expands on a grammatical point (ex: pronoun forms, verb tenses, plurality) or grammatical structure (ex: word order, subject-verb agreement) encountered in the reading. All three exercises require the students to examine the details of the reading passage.

Using the Books

The format of the four-book series is simple and easy to use, allowing for its use by individuals working in an independent mode or by students in a teacher-guided formal class.

Independent Study Mode.

The answers in the back of the book allow learners to work on their language skills completely independently or to use the material as a supplement to a formal study program. The 160 units in the complete series give self-studying learners sufficient material for several hours of study. The progression of the units from short to longer passages provides controlled challenge and comprehensible input. As the passages increase in length and in vocabulary level, the learners' "known" language also increases to meet the challenge of dealing with the "unknowns" of the passages. The uniformity of the units allows the learners the opportunity to focus on the language and not waste time trying to figure out what to do from unit to unit. Most important, perhaps, by following through the entire series, the learners will experience the satisfaction of feeling and recognizing progress.

Formal Class Mode.

Using the books as part of ongoing class work can be done in a variety of ways. A simple and effective procedure is outlined below:

1) Pre-reading preparation. Introduce the nature of the topic and engage the students in a discussion or question-answer session that activates what they may already know about the topic.

2) Initial, silent reading. The students read the passage silently with (or without, as you prefer) their dictionaries to gain an overall understanding. Depending on the level of the class, one to three minutes should be sufficient for this.

3) Reading aloud. This can be done by the teacher, or by students taking turns. A pause for questions and clarification can be added after each sentence or only after the entire passage.

4) Doing the exercises. This can be done individually, but it is often more effective to pair the students and have them work cooperatively. Simply put, two heads are better than one, and the practice of working and learning together can be a very valuable learning experience in itself.

5) Checking the answers. Self-checking or paired checking may generate some questions which should be clarified either as a whole-class activity or as the teacher circulates and responds to individuals or pairs.

6) Discussion. A teacher-led or small-group discussion of the content gives the students the opportunity to use the language they already command to talk about new information with newly acquired knowledge and skill (new words, phrases, structures).

7) Writing. The students can keep a notebook or journal and record a sentence or two, ("Today, I learned . ."), or perhaps a paragraph stimulated by the reading. An alternative is to do a short dictation using sentences based on the information in the reading.

Semi-Independent Study.

The material can be used in a formal program by having the students read the material and do the exercises out of class. For example, a unit is assigned for homework, and is followed by a brief review the next day. An alternative is a teacher-made quiz to keep the students on task.

Using the CD

A CD is available for each book. It is an optional element, but its use may provide an important and valuable extra dimension to the reading program. Obviously, the CD offers an opportunity for the students to hear a standard pronunciation and phrasing of the text. This can be a very important supplement to an independent study mode, and it may also be very useful in a setting where the teacher's own pronunciation is too heavily influenced by their native language. The CD can also be used to work on listening comprehension. It can be played in class before or after the reading, or the students can follow along by looking at the text as they listen.

Legends: 52 People Who Made a Difference

Graded readings from American history – beginner to intermediate. There are 13 units, each with four readings of 100, 150, 200, and 250 words. The legendary people covered in the units are folk heroes, Civil War and anti-slavery heroes, Native Americans, inventors and scientists, educators and reformers, adventurers, human rights leaders, business and labor leaders, famous presidents, military leaders and heroes, writers, entertainers, and sports heroes. Personal and historical time lines are designed for controlled practice of language structures and to stimulate conversation about American culture and history. CD available.

American Holidays: Exploring Traditions, Customs, & Backgrounds

An intermediate reader explaining each of the official national holidays, three cultural holidays (Chinese New Year, Kwanzaa, and Cinco de Mayo), and Christian, Muslim, and Jewish religious holidays. Exercises practice vocabulary building skills, discussion, and Web research. CD available.

Surveys for Conversation

48 surveys designed for beginning to intermediate students – before class they read the surveys and fill them out with their personal information and opinions. In class they enjoy lively conversations which everyone is prepared to participate in. Topics include family, friendship, pets, shopping, clothes, TV, music, computers, space, celebrations, love, marriage, birth & death, work, books, health, summer, winter, crime, war & peace, AD 2100, and the environment.

Do As I Say: Operations, Procedures, and Rituals

A TPR classic revised and updated. Fun activities are ideal for building vocabulary, confidence with grammar, and accuracy in giving and taking instructions.

The Sanchez Family: Now, Tomorrow, and Yesterday

A first book for beginning ESL/EFL students which in a few pages teaches three survival tenses: present progressive, going-to future, and past.

English Interplay

Beginning to intermediate texts for basic English, focused primarily on interactive activities in the classroom using many different approaches and techniques to build vocabulary and all language skills.

To order or for information on these and other materials, contact

www.ProLinguaAssociates.com or 800-366-4775